THE SEA CHEST

THE SEA CHEST

KERRY GREER

RECENT
WORK
PRESS

The Sea Chest
Recent Work Press
Canberra, Australia

Copyright © Kerry Greer, 2023

ISBN: 9780645651331 (paperback)

 A catalogue record for this
book is available from the
National Library of Australia

Cover image: Pawel Czerwinski via unsplash;
            internal image © Caitlin McGregor, 2023
Cover design: Recent Work Press
Set by Recent Work Press

recentworkpress.com

PL

For Gabriel—I will be listening for your voice until I see you again.

For Raphael—My sun, my moon, my stars.

Contents

HORIZON-MIRAGE

INTO HALF-LIGHT

Fire lives the death of earth, as air
lives the death of fire.

Heraclitus, *Fragments*

Although the wind
blows terribly here
the moonlight also leaks
between the roof planks
of this ruined house.

Izumi Shikibu, *Although the wind*
(transl. Jane Hirshfield)

Preface

On the morning of September 8, 2017, my husband Gabriel ended his own life by multiple means after a long struggle with chronic headaches. He was 32, and I was 29. In the days before his death, Gabriel had commenced treatment with high-dose, intravenous ketamine. He'd served as a U.S. Marine in his twenties, and he heard about this treatment through a support network for veterans. The headaches started after a car accident in 2009 and never improved. We travelled the world to see specialists across the spectrum of Western and Eastern medicine, even living with shaman in the Amazon at one point. Gabriel's death came as an immense shock to me and all who knew him. Although he experienced 24/7 headaches, he had been optimistic that we would find a solution. I loved him so much that I felt I was in it with him. I wanted him to know, always, that he wasn't alone, that we wouldn't stop searching until we found the right doctor, the right treatment. And if the treatment hadn't been invented yet, we would wait for it, together. When Gabriel decided to end his life, he did it on the first attempt. He didn't hint at the extreme nature of his plans. He made sure there could be no chance of survival.

Years later, I'm still coming to terms with the loss. I have his ashes beside my bed, yet I think I'll see him again. The grief makes me crazy in ways only I can know: Of course he can't come back. Of course he might hear me saying this, might find a way to send a sign, if I listen carefully. Because of this incongruity—because I choose negative capability over the idea that he is gone forever—I can keep going. Grief creates a double-life that the grieving rarely talk about because it persists inside the mind. Nothing about this is straightforward, and the circumstances of Gabriel's death only add to the ambiguity and uncertainty I carry forward.

Gabriel and I had lived together in Albuquerque, New Mexico, where he grew up. We met in 2010 when Gabriel was an exchange student at the University of Western Australia. From a chance encounter in the student administration building, we talked for three hours. He was unlike anyone I had met before. When his student visa to Australia expired, he casually suggested that I should apply for a fiancée visa to the U.S. The visa process was a lengthy one. I wasn't allowed to visit the U.S. on a tourist visa because I'd shown intent to immigrate, so we met overseas multiple times, waiting to hear the outcome of my visa application. Every time we had to say goodbye, I was so distressed I felt physically unwell.

On that Friday in September 2017, Gabriel left our apartment around 9 a.m., carrying his lunch in a glass container and two large bottles of alkaline water. He had taken the previous week off work to undergo treatment with IV ketamine—a treatment he cut short as it had increased his pain and caused an array of other unexpected side effects, including paranoia and insomnia. For days, I hadn't let Gabriel out of my sight. I drove him everywhere he needed to go, and included him in everything I did with Raphael. By Thursday that week, Gabriel seemed to be feeling more normal, and he was eager to return to his job at a local cardiac rehabilitation clinic. The nurse practitioner who had administered the ketamine assured Gabriel he was fine to resume regular activities. We were under the impression the effects of ketamine would diminish within a few days.

At first, Gabriel had rushed out of our apartment that morning without saying goodbye. This wasn't his usual behaviour, but he had seemed distracted, not his cheerful, funny self. He said he wanted to stop by his parents' house on the way to work. They were away at a health retreat, and Gabriel was worried they might have left the water for their evaporative cooler running. He was proactive in caring for the environment, and this explanation made sense to me. Our 18-month-old son, Raphael, started crying as soon as Gabriel left, so I called from the doorway to Gabriel, asking him to return. He walked back down the hallway and kissed Raphael's head once, for a long moment. Raphael then wrapped his arms around Gabriel's head and said 'Love,' which was one of his favourite words in this time. I don't remember if Gabriel kissed me. I only remember the feeling of holding Raphael up to Gabriel.

When the door closed again, Raphael banged his head into a wall, crying and running around in distress. This, too, wasn't Raphael's normal behaviour. I picked him up and we went to the balcony, which overlooked our parked car. We heard the entrance doors to the apartment building open below us. I lifted Raphael and held him against my shoulder, so that he could wave to Gabriel on the footpath. As Gabriel passed our balcony, I noticed he was talking to himself, but I couldn't hear what he was saying. Once he reached our car, he looked up and smiled, his face briefly untroubled. 'I'll see you tonight, beautiful,' he called. Then he started the car and drove away. As if caught in the camera's flash, certain images never leave my mind. Other parts are blind spots, redacted—black gaps in time.

After Gabriel left, I moved from room to room of our apartment, sometimes looking outside at the road and the row of pine trees next to our windows. The trees cast long shadows over the grass below. Cars passed by every so often. It was a quiet day, an Indian summer descending slowly through the air. The sun shone on the adobe clay of the house across the road. But on our side of the street, no sunlight pierced the foliage. Inside our apartment, I was unable to remain still. I felt cold all over, tense with anxiety, but I couldn't pinpoint a particular cause. I distracted myself by making breakfast for Raphael. I decided to take him to a park, yet I was unable to focus my energy on leaving. I walked into the bathroom to start getting ready, and stared at myself in the mirror, then walked out. I picked up my phone and tried to call Gabriel, though there was nothing I needed to tell him. He didn't answer, and I paced through the apartment. I set my phone down in the bathroom. I went to check on Raphael, then heard my phone ringing. I thought it must be Gabriel returning my call, but it was a friend who lived next-door to Gabriel's parents. She said that Gabriel's parents' house was on fire. Our car was parked outside. She said several times: 'The fire department is already there. I'm sure he will be ok.' The facts moved apart like water vapour in my mind. A fire. Our car. He should be at work by now. His parents' house. But he was at work. We would see him after he finished work.

My limbs seemed held together only by my skin. I carried Raphael down the long hallway of the apartment complex to the car we had borrowed from Gabriel's parents. I remember starting to cry. I remember trembling all over, pressing Raphael against my chest to steady my hands. I buckled him into his car-seat. I drove at high speed, weaving in and out of traffic on the freeway. I wanted the police to pull us over, to take us to the house with sirens ringing, so everyone would move out of our way. I called Gabriel maybe eight times while driving like this. If I turned my head very slightly to the left, I could see smoke rising through the air, hanging in a low cloud over the neighbourhood where my parents-in-law lived. Of course I already knew. I knew back in the apartment—unable to run, unable to be still. An hour after Gabriel left for work, he was dead. His death certificate lists a combination of stab wounds, thermal wounds, and smoke inhalation as the cause(s) of death. He had also attempted to hang himself. Official documents cannot capture the chaos I walked into, when I was later allowed inside the burnt-out house. There, in the kitchen, beside the stove, where we had so often stood together talking, cooking, kissing—a grey space, the shape and length of his body. And all around, black. And all inside, black.

Following Gabriel's death, I returned to my family in Perth with Raphael. The singular force which carried me through the shock was Raphael. Caring for him necessitated acts of love across days, weeks, months. If I was heavy with grief or loneliness, he needed me—needed some very real and urgent thing from me—and I could never stop for long to think about my shock or despair. In this way, years have passed. And my son—he is exceptional. He comes from some other place: the place where words originate, where Gabriel might also be. To live only with a child is to live in a world of miracles, of small and holy moments that unfold as seamlessly as a chain of paper dolls.

The poetry collection that follows addresses what it is like to live without Gabriel. Grief is not fixed in time: it deepens over years, privately, in the ordinary moments that form a life. I circle the edges of his absence, trying to perceive him in shadow and in grey—where he might be, what he might say or do—because the cord of shared existence, of devotion, cannot be cut as easily, as swiftly, as a life departs. In this way, it can feel as if Gabriel is still here—as if we are still in conversation, but his answers come from very far away, by diffuse means. So, I make a life of listening, of solitude, of belief in what I cannot know for sure. His absence is a sort of presence, too—the gap left by someone who was vivid and real, and who, somehow, might return soon.

BLACK TIDE

And the flame of the blue star of twilight, hung low on the rim of the sky,
Has awakened in our hearts, my beloved, a sadness that may not die.
> W.B. Yeats, *The White Birds*

I would have loved him
in any era, in any dark age
> Dorianne Laux, *As It Is*

Questions

The map was a body
And it all went up in flames.

> Yes, that's right, I have his ashes,
> Mostly here. Some were given

I can't tell you favourite landmarks
Anymore. I liked all of it.

> To his brother and his sisters,
> To his mother and his father.

There was a place I often visited.
My son was with me. When I dream,

> We walked his favourite trail, the
> Piedra Lisa, and scattered his ashes.

I can find my way there again.
There are cottonwoods, wild clematis.

> The wind blew the ashes against
> My face, into my hair. I remembered

Next to a field, Ojito de San Antonio,
I often see a man. He is facing

> Lying with my head on his chest
> In the night, the way he smelled of cedar.

Away from me, into the wind.
Sometimes when my son looks

> I keep the rest in a box next to my bed.
> The wind doesn't get a second chance.

9

Down at me, from his bed, I think:
This is the face of the man.

When I flew with his ashes from New Mexico
To Australia, the Customs Officer asked me:

The child will turn, and there
The map will be.

What is in this heavy box? My sister-in-law
Talked for me. Everyone else was quiet.

In a box, I have a map.
On the bed, sleeping

Scales tilted like a compass. The airport turned
Its eyes on me: the person with the heavy box.

There is a small boy.
He will know the way.

Rain Lilies

I.

The problem was,
I could never say no to him, not
out of motherly concern or
a sense of duty. Certainly

those were there, but only in
a dormant sense, kicking in
late like a door coming off its hinges
in a storm. No,

I could never say no to him
for a different reason.

Have you ever seen flowers—
rain lilies, for example—
come back to life after
almost-death?

Have you seen the owner of the flowers—
a neighbour, perhaps—
in the garden on warm evenings,
water falling from a mint-green
watering can across the soil.
And he is pleased. He has had
a long day, and now
he breathes. There is the sky,
he says, without opening his mouth.
The flowers never turn their faces
away from him. Always they are looking
up. Waiting.

Through the window, later,
the man is visible, pressing
a crease into grey slacks.
The lights go out. The lilies
are as close and as far
from the window as they
will ever be.

Days pass, half-light hits
the tinted glass, reflecting back
the outside world, scudding cloud
and something darker than blue,
which is the sky looking
at itself.

Every leaf in the garden might
have blown to the corners
against the fence.
But the rain lilies
are still, almost somehow
taller. Watching.

So my son was unwell.
So he was almost better.
So he said—
Mommy, can I sleep next to you?
Can I have an extra day at home?

What do the specifics matter?
I let everything fall apart
because I liked to be near him,
to watch his face watching the sky
after long days inside, unwell,
the curtains drawn.

A moon, a sun, a thimble of
light moving back and forth, ceaseless,
sharp as the axis of Death
on which Life spins, turns, catches
glimpses of its eternal shape
in lovely, smaller things, repeated—
days, or children, or the softest word:
yes,
yes, that will be ok,
my darling.

II.

Once I almost died.
I saw the moment moving past me like a white cloud
sucked into a storm. Yes, I might go too.

My husband burned alive. I want to tell you this. This is the hinge
giving way. What he did and I'll never know—
did he really want that, so much more than us?

But I only watched the cloud pass,
and when I opened my eyes,
my child was there. His child.
This boy so like him.
Except for his eyes, which are
the colour of the sky

holding everything.

I could wake every day
to him, to his vast needs
framed in simple terms.
An extra day together—
wasn't that just life?
Just day after day after day?

How could I say no?
Let the rest fall away as
rain. I was nobody's wife—
I was only his mother.
I might stretch forever
when
he looked back at me.

Hunter Green

The jungle feasts on fallen fruit, undulating hunger.
Everything is green, growing and dying,
the land changing daily in the ceaseless rain.
The dead are buried and, still, come back to life.

Everything is green, growing and dying,
in that teeming space, life erupting from decay.
The dead are buried and, still, come back to life.
There is no map to show what lies within the soil.

In that teeming space, life erupting from decay,
I heard you screaming, tied down by dreams
buried in the soil of yourself, a land without a map,
and no way out, no way up, to the air, the light.

I heard you screaming, tied down by dreams
of childhood, of some black seed at the centre,
and no way out, no way up, to the air, the light.
As with any flooded place, decay grew from the roots—

from childhood, from some black seed at the centre.
You asked me later what I had dreamed, and I didn't answer.
As with any flooded place, decay grew from the roots.
How could I have slept, while next to me you screamed?

You asked me later what I had dreamed, and I looked away.
The hands of vines moved over us, blocking out the night.
I can say it now: I dreamed that you were dying.
Tell me where this leads, I'm asking for a compass,

some way to navigate the moving dark, the hands of vines
that catch me in my dreams again, again blocking out the light.

Tell me where this leads, I have lost my compass.
Where you walked is gone, is sliding towards the river.

Caught in dreams without you, without the light,
the land turns its face from me, refuses to be mapped.
Where you walked is gone, is sliding towards the river,
smooth as a hunter snaking through the leaves.

The land turns its face from me, refuses to be mapped.
I slip down, find vines waiting there
sharp as a hunter snaking through the leaves.
One thousand shades of green, and every shade decays.

I slip down, find vines waiting there
to bury me, my footprints swallowed by the rain.
One thousand shades of green, and every shade decays.
I move through sleep to find you, and always I'm too late.

Buried, no footprints to follow in the rain,
where you walked is gone, and you are gone as well.
I move through sleep to find you, and always I'm too late,
waking to find the dream was not a dream.

Where you walked is gone, and you are gone as well,
the land changing daily in the ceaseless rain.
The dream was not a dream. Awake,
the jungle feasts on fallen fruit, undulating hunger.

Lake

I don't want to let anyone else in
yet
but I remember being loved
the slope of your shoulder
as you pressed
                          forward and I
yielded, my hands knowing
the movement of your back

not
ever from sight
as now I watch outside the
memory a lurker
awkward and real

your love was felt
as safety as a rush

a ripple carried from your shoulders
all the way down my spine—

and they say you are so far
away you won't be coming
back   is it strange that

sometimes all of me

is very still
is hushed as
lake becoming glass

but look—

there
softly
like a shiver
the water, watch closely
it moves—

tell me how the wind works
why is it like being touched
pressed close
all the way up
my skin
to the nape of—

no tell me instead
what do you hold
where you are
so far away?

Object Permanence

I.

We bought picture books. He learned by observation
as well. I don't remember telling him his father was dead—
that's not a word like *ball* or *milk* or *rattle*.
It can't be attached to anything. The thing it is attached to is going,
is already gone. The books on grief advised against
euphemisms like *passed away* or *with the angels*.
Everything needed to be literal, real, rooted to the ground
when talking to a child. That child might think Heaven is a real place—
the yellow clapboard house next-door perhaps, or the ocean
at low-tide, at sunset, at the red edge of the reef—a place from which
someone could return. Children see dreams all the time, and we call this
imagination. We draw a line, flat as the horizon. Some things
you're not allowed to say you've seen. But—

like a fish
pulled by a hook
something sharp inside me moved—
    dead?
The word cut me to pieces when I tried to
speak it. Take the word away
gently. Do not go near my child.

Over and over, we studied one particular book:
When somebody dies, their body is broken
and cannot be fixed. A robot was in pieces
in the picture. This was the sticking point:
was it truly impossible to put the robot back together?
That, he said, pointing. *That, that, that.* He was 18 months old.
We spoke the same language of uncomprehending
shock. That, that, that. The book fell open onto
that page, that day and the next day, and the next, and the next—

There was a way to explain it without sitting him down
and saying, *Your father has died in a fire.* What I have seen,
nobody wants to hear.

He put his arms around me when I cried.
He said, *Love.* He tried many times to pick me up.
He was very small. I remember his arms around my back.
I remember the tiles, the feeling I had cracked.

II.

One day, months after the event, he stood beside the car,
looking up, eyes narrowed: *Daddy—in the sky?* he asked.
I stopped at the front door, the key pointed towards
the lock. I said, *Which adult used those words
to you? Daddy isn't in the sky.*
He can't come back.
And my son kept staring up, trying
to figure out the way a man might fly,
There, Mommy, look—

I watched his face as if a vast
door was opening.
His eyes tracked movement—the line
of a lure hooked on something
solid and
impossible.

I knelt beside him then.
I held him by his shoulders.
I moved my face close to his.
I said, *What was he wearing?*
Did he have wings?
I want to see him too.
Point, my darling.
Please, I want to see him too—

Once

I.

I went to South Korea with a man I loved.

Years after that, I watched a movie about a murder
that took place in Seoul,
the whole time saying:
> let it go let it go this isn't about him

I turned the movie off and realised
even the darkness of the room
was about him.

There was nowhere we would go together
again, so I turned the movie back on—
only to see the red-brick streets, the back
of a man walking along
before he knew he might die,
his head innocently curious as he passed
a BBQ restaurant or a hole-in-the-wall noodle shop,
glancing in the window, the lovely symmetry
of his profile, and me behind
a step or two

in the living room.

II.

I watched a movie about a murder that took place in Seoul.

Years before, I had been there with my husband.
The streets of Sinchon near the university were familiar.

I was walking there again in the movie
in my mind with this man. It was not a lonely place anymore
in my living room. The darkness moved
about me like the screen of time crumpling to the floor—
a sheet, a flimsy thing, a film still
you can see through.

Look closely. We are about to cross the road, leaving
Dongdaemun Market, where I bought navy stockings and later
cut the feet off them, calling them *leggings* because I had no trousers,
because I was too cold and too tall everywhere we went, because we arrived
in Seoul wearing flip-flops on a whim on a flight from summer
in northern Thailand. (The way we lived, like we knew
we wouldn't do it twice.) For a moment, the traffic is far away,
a flat block of champagne-white headlights
blending in with the machinery of this smooth, un-
blemished city. There is no rubbish; there are
no rubbish bins. Everyone waits for the Green Man
to lead us across the road. There is no jaywalking;
there is no wayward American saying:
*Come on, baby, maybe we'll end up in a high-tech
Korean jail.* It's a movie.

But some nights I see him at my periphery
on the streets that line my living room
with places I have been, some nights
smell the bibimbap
cooking just
                    over there, feel somebody run
across the pavement inside my chest—
a little shiver, a little shock, like:
*How dare he do that. How dare he just keep
going—*

22

The Ferry

On Sundays, my father would take us on a ferry that cruised
    the Swan River, away from the city towards the Indian Ocean.

At a certain beautiful house along the river's edge—
    a cream-pink orthogonal dream of stucco, an infinity pool

cascading not quite to the collarbone of rock and sand below,
    and a wrought iron fence sealing in the scene—

the ferry would turn around, so that we never reached the sea.
    A tour guide talked of the sights along the river's edge,

of a horse taken by a bull-shark in the shallows, of the people
    who built mansions beside the water. This was the 1990s,

and our history lesson was incomplete, but it took me years
    to realise this. We travelled on the ferry almost weekly, going

nowhere, and I thought that it was normal. Maybe I assumed
    it was inexpensive, or I didn't think at all about the money,

the real price of the tickets. I was on the outside of something—
    looking in—my whole life, moving countries or suburbs

sometimes monthly, not so different from the tourists in bum-bags,
    their fluoro jackets crinkling like candy wrappers in the wind

rippling off the water. When we were on top of the river,
    I could see it was always moving. But from far away,

it had seemed like a glass tabletop I might cross by foot
    if I moved quickly enough. At a kiosk inside the ferry,

my father would buy tea and a plate of Monte Carlos
      for my brothers and me, then he'd put his sunglasses on

and close his eyes for a minute or two, leaning his head back
      and breathing deeply, his arms folded, his lips pressed

flat. The repose of the grim, the ill-at-ease. But sometimes,
      his body would be turned towards the window,

and when I studied him, I would see his eyes moving
      across the water and the land, alert. How I wanted

to know him. There was never any way to reach inside
      to the person below the surface—the one who needed

to close his eyes to the light, take us on ferry rides week
      after week as if we might keep going—going into

open water. My brothers and I would leave a trail
      of tea and soggy crumbs beside him, walking outside

to the deck to spot jellyfish or lean over the railing,
      our fingers stretching down towards the whitewash

and the deep. The movement of the sun across the water
      was like a marble, rolling on and on, always just out of reach.

Most of all, I loved to look at the sharp houses along the cliffs,
      their tennis courts that might tumble into the river

if pride and bad weather conspired. My father said we'd buy
      a yacht, learn to sail, and I would be the lookout

because of my excellent eyesight. All the ways he wanted
      to run, and still I couldn't see it.

A few months later, we waited in a yellow room with steel gates
    to see my father.

I watched as my brothers' bodies were scanned, patted down,
    pockets checked for sticks, rocks, razors, drugs,

their dark heads turning to my mother, who held my baby brother
    and our whole world together, her jaw set like a steel trap

and somehow her eyes still kind. I was patted down too, then
    we were allowed to hug my father. At a table, our favourite crisps

and cans of soft drink waited. We sat on scratched plastic chairs
    beside a window, a view of the sand, the scrub—the inland

desert of this country where you'd die if you tried to run.
    In the window, I would follow my father's eyes moving past

my mother and the baby, to the sky and the fence outside.
    And again, the longing to see beyond the glass,

the feeling I was looking into a mirror from far away
    when I found his eyes looking back.

Ghost Tongue

I.

Go inside and undo
                    this terrible
mess I've made,
I said to the pills in my hand.
And they went inside,
                    and everything
was calm, was still.

Later, into my hand,
I spat a peach
                    pit, serrated,
fresh crimson,
as if just recently
                    sucked,
not yet dry.
Inside I was raw, cut blush.

Someone had forced
                    a sharp thing
through
                    my throat
to see the empty
                    space
inside.

At my feet, limp flesh
                    bitter,
tang of blood leaking
                    bright.

After that
               the pills
I didn't tell anything
             at all.
I couldn't say anything
             at all
I felt.

I felt nothing at all.
I said:
             I felt nothing.
I didn't stutter.

I didn't talk.
I didn't write.
          The pills
were calm.
          I was still.

If later
I tried to remember
           how
to try
          to speak
a breeze whistled
          not like
a train pushing through
a tunnel to the lip
of light outside

just the
          shivers
of a draught rasping through

a flatland,
cleared even of
the soil.

II.

But the sounds
howling through that place
when the sun is gone. Like a far-
off voice trying to say:
I do not feel well.
I want to be allowed out of here, this dark room in the basement wing,
long and airless, hidden limb of a crushed dove: Ward D.
What did it all mean? The Psychiatric Ward, the place I would get
better, go home from, never to return? And Dr. Claussens with his
thick hair slicked back, shining dark
as leather boots, asking if I liked the food, the bed,
the treatment plan—throaty Afrikaans cracking
through the seams of polite conversation:

There is a girl in here, like you. She did not cooperate.
She threw herself into the walls, and I told her:
'We will have to use ECT. There will be no choice.'

I remembered the girl's voice, distant knife of air
travelling around corners, days ago.

Cold down here without the sunlight.
The white, white walls, the locked
doors, the windows that
aren't there.

Through the curtain around my bed,
I hear my room-mate rolling over,
rustle of wrappers—maybe chocolate,
maybe a sponge-cake from the vending machine

glistening like a pearl forever
the same shade. Her lamp goes on.
It is night-time with the strip lights
off, but she wants company.

She says, *I wish I had your problem.*
I can't stop eating. And I coil around
my empty stomach, the iron part of me
> that does not break
> that will not be broken,
like hugging a broad steel bollard,
the rim pressing into my chest
where the loneliness goes numb.

> We were somewhere else down there
> in the Public Hospital
> > Psychiatric Ward.
> We'd fallen forty years through
> the floor. The corridors were tunnels,
> were sound-proofed by cement.
> If I said, *I didn't think things like this happened anymore,*
> the nurses laughed. I'd been too long in the air
> up there, they replied in scalpelled smiles—
> *Oh sweetheart, oh silly starving thing.*

My room-mate sighs, turns out the light.
I breathe deeply and pretend to sleep
in the moonless dark on my side
of the curtain. How long this night,
how far away the duck pond where I walked
days ago, and kept walking, and kept
walking, until I was across the road
in pyjamas, testing the length of the rope.

Sounds from the outside world echo
through the elevator shaft near our room,

regret moving slowly towards the heart.
In the night, I dream of the duck pond—
that it is not so far away, that I might cross it
and not return. In my dreams, always the beeping
of the hospital at rest, red flash of someone pleading
at waist-height—the way the ear creates an image
of who is standing, who is lying down—

> *Please let me walk to the pond*
> *tomorrow—I will take*
> *the medication—I can't remember*
> *why I refused*
> *anymore I can't remember—*

and the quiet afterwards, the white night
of the dreamless sleep.
Dr. Claussens in the morning, checking on me,
checking my clothing for food I had hidden
on my person. *Empty your pockets.*
I smile. I open my mouth so he knows
I've swallowed everything; all that food
they call medicine.
Hospital white bread and hospital green jelly
on hospital melamine plates. *Good girl*, he says.
You can go to the bathroom now.

Down the long white hall, I am trusted
just this far. Yesterday, a nurse escorted me
everywhere—my voyeur, eyes
downcast as she asked me to strip, to step
onto the scales. The stale brown of her coffee breath,
her hands sliding down my hips
into my pockets. *You lot are the most difficult,*
the most resistant, she had whispered,
checking for uneaten meals hidden in my clothes.
We let you out and you try to run.
Just look at you. You're sick.
I had studied my wrists then,

the blue lines of personal space.
No windows, no mirrors, no glass
of any kind, but her disgust slicing
across my skin. *I didn't run,*
I came back, I wanted to say, but I held
my breath, tried not to breathe her in.

Today, I am allowed to be alone.
I might be anywhere
                    in my head
that is not here.

Everything is bright
and cold and lovely
                    as I walk
down the hallway
                    into the sea
going under
                    to the silence
and the rush of
                    water on my hands.

Wash six times. Every time,
forget
                    forget that it was done, forget
where you are,
                    start again all over from
the start again all over
                    from the start
again a fresh, clean thing
                    to be folded up
and put away
                    inside a cupboard
under the stairs.

Not six times but
six perfect times
later, I return to my bed,
listen to the air
moving through the elevator shaft.

32

blackberry, blackberry, black—

The candle that cannot be burned
again, not trusted to the air. Covered in blue cloth.
Dried hollyhock taped to the glass container, and the wick excised.
Inside, resting on the cold wax: spearhead relic from Mezquital
desert and a cufflink your grandfather wore. You saying:
He gave them to me when he was alive. The boy picking
something up from the ground, a treasure pocketed as if
a gift. That came into my head, knowing you, knowing
boys. Walking into the bedroom once in a hurry to reach for
a clean bib, seeing this candle burning on the window sill,
the wind toying with the flame. You said you'd met a man
selling ideas of financial freedom, and you'd come away
with this homemade candle, two days before my birthday.
This, the only present you gave me proudly,
not leading with: *I'm terrible at choosing gifts.*

Returning upstairs to the baby
calling for me with his thumps that might be
a vase falling, or his body rolling off the couch,
then back down the stairs to our bedroom for the forgotten bib—
Suddenly, the glass burning black and the head of
hollyhock aflame, mesmerising as it caught
the light, the hand of wind coming through the window, commanding
this way, that way, further, turn—
The room billowing with the scent of
lavender and iris, like breathing in the blue notes
of a lullaby. Long
pause before I stepped towards the bathroom, those cups of water
you left everywhere in the house—just what I needed.
Would I have done a thing like that?
Would I have left a candle burning unattended
in those newborn days, days of endless waking?

Sometimes exhaustion feels very like standing still
and watching everyone else live—
if only they would leave the room, carry with them all that noise,
slide slim packets of caffeine tablets under the door.

I took the baby out in the pram one day, found a new flower
to press and dry, tape against the glass, make right
mistakes I don't remember making. Cut the wick
to the root so nobody could finish what I started.

Some other man picked the candle up years later
in my bedroom
and I watched him as if he held my baby
in his giant, clumsy hands, no idea
of how a head can fall under its own weight.
He examined the spear-flint and cufflink,
half-smile tilted towards me like I was the curiosity, to keep
these sharp things hidden there on the indigo wax.
Under his thumb—the black cloud along the glass,
a bruise where my whole life might have come undone.

I took the candle from him,
slipped myself between his hands instead,
pushed the blackened glass and its treasures back
into the dark along the edge of the drawers.

Someone gave the spearhead and cufflink to me,
I said. And he didn't care,
pressed me closer to the wall
with the glass at my back
and his tongue moving
this way, that way, further in
making me curl, contort
like I was a scrap of straw and
any old flame would do.

The See-Through Friend

I met a man who said,
You drive me crazy,
and I made of him
a real God, fleshy, not in the subjunctive.

I messaged Him, *I'm free until 1:30pm,*
and He replied at 1:29pm, telling me to
come now or not at all—
knowing I liked the slim gaps best, the parts that
were as needles to pass through.

When I arrived, I undressed carefully before His eyes,
lacquered in false calm, having rushed the whole way
there. We floated separately in His backyard
swimming pool, Him pushing water with His hands
and talking, talking like He'd never held
a dialogue. I lay back and studied the vaulted
sky, a scarlet robin in flight. He spoke of His plans
for His garden, how He wanted cuttings
from my bougainvillea bush, and—
would I like some hanging bottlebrush in exchange?
None of these things were awful euphemisms
because He was innocent as the milk-eyed moon, watching
all and seeing nothing, especially not me, almost naked
floating past His arms, His feet. An arborist, and
a narcissist perhaps—in the blameless way of
an only child or a Hollywood star—but nothing worse.

Briefly, I closed my eyes and sank my head under
the water, feeling silence move across my neck, my lips.
Then I rose from the pool, told God I needed to leave.
I walked across His jarrah floorboards without a towel.
We have no chemistry, I said. *I'm not attracted to you.*

He looked down at His body—golden
with self-belief and all that time in His garden—
breathing fast as if struck by a blunt object.

You drive me crazy, He said again and
          pressed Himself against my cold skin.
For a moment I let Him do as He pleased,
this impossible God. He lifted my hair
from the nape of my neck, twisting it
so that I was contorted, forced to breathe in the vapour
rising off His shoulders, salt and chlorine all along
my cheek. *I have to pick my son up now.*
He will be waiting for me, I said, moving away
as glass flying from His hand, walking barefoot across
His perfect grass. He let it happen then—let me
leave, even opening my car-door, suddenly courteous.
As He did, a red balloon my son kept
like a see-through friend
floated out of the car, in a hurry
to some better place, exhaling
far

          away. At the school gates, my son stood
alone, sharp-eyed as a rock
under whitewash. He studied the empty
space where his balloon had been. The night before,
he had drawn two irregular eyes on the balloon,
and a wide smile, the sort you make
when staggering off a rollercoaster, asking
to go for a second time, a third time, and again
just one more ride, please, Mommy—
miraculous to be so free, a small
god rising red-cheeked
into the sky—

and all the world below you
hanging by a thread.

Trinity

The opposite of God:

His absence. I can curl my body
                around the space, make myself

a vast devil missing all the good
                parts, and still they say I'm not enough:

He's bigger than
                this grief. See though,

the grief: it makes me cruel,
                makes me say things I can't mean,

loudly. What of words, what of
                how the lips are like a hole

in the weft of the body, cleaving
                as wool to let night through?

I told a man who was good to me
                that I didn't love him.

I even said: *I never loved you.*
                I watched confusion twist to the hilt

in his stomach. Two years he waited,
                because it helped me

to keep him there, to keep him
                in your shadow, all of us waiting.

I did this same thing,
                several times over to different men.

They were not you, and it was important
                I cut them off, especially before September 8.

I pressed my face against a keyhole
                of darkness, saying softly again and

again: *I made a mistake. Let's try one more time—*
                And always, I was calling out

to you, my Love. Your absence
                cannot be fixed with thoughts

and prayers. It drinks the marrow
                from my bones, leaves gaps

inside, a sucking noise. Listen now,
                lie very still, as you do so well:

I know you're in the room with me.
                I hear you best

when nobody is near us, and you touch
                gently the space inside

my chest, which never hurts like this
                when you are far away, and

I am alone. I have loved such things as rup-
                ture, as exile, my secret

second moon, because
                all the time it hurts this much,

I'm getting closer
                getting closer to you.

Line Feed 07-09-2021

*Imagine a planet where the past never went away
but kept happening again and again, forever.*
          Richard Powers, *Bewilderment*

My hands mark prayers in keys, mark mantras
without beads, asking for a loophole, for divine
return: return again to me.

Caution tape surrounds the fragile parts.
It wasn't only you who died there behind
the line of orange
and black, which someone lifted for me
so I could pass beneath to reach you,
as if I wasn't already with you inside
on the floor. Tell me where to draw the line.
I lose track of time, feel it slipping through

my hands, rope-burn tracks map
how hope slips beyond
my grasp.
                    Four years ago, the middle
               of my life became also an end,
          cartridge return that I can't mend

bleeding full stops like blank shots. Return.
Return again. I'm stuck speaking this same line
like the seasons repeating the refrain of last year,
or four years before
when you first died, loaded spring
uncoiling and then the long
recoil, hard into my chest as if I held
the gun.
                    All the words I write to you,
I cannot swallow them into the ouro-
boros of my body, a benign lump

in my lungs. Carry them away
yourself or mark them with invisible ink
across your now
invisible skin. I cannot do everything
alone.
This is enough for me to bear:

today is the day before
you died
again.
I bury you a second time with my guilt,
a third with every new man I cut
off, and a fourth when I convince
your son that a father in spirit
is still a father in blood.
I invoke the name of Christ for him,
your son. My God, my love:
look what you have done.

September 7, and I ask for death:
tomorrow.
The anger, it might choke. Send me
a target to mark with my rope, the line
I cannot find. I am dying too today.
I want so much
to take others down with me.
I remember once I could be kind, and
I remember all the ways you died,
all the ways I fell in love with other
men and could not let it pass.
How I stuttered-shuddered-staggered forward
jagged as the breaking of a
line, thud of body falling
in love: same sound as my heart beating
blunt in panic seeking you year on year on

                                on repeat up here.

And you down in the earth, the roughness
of you that catches at my throat, the way
it feels to drop hard against a rope.

I split my tongue when I swore
you'd be the only one.
Send every other love away.
Return again to that first line:
I only asked for you.

On the Third Day

I.

The work of the flesh,
the desire to be next to God
so I can be nearer to you,
cleaned of what I've done
in your absence.

These things are never finished,
doing
pressing into
undoing,
undressing
to hide
in nakedness in darkness
on the bed
what should not see the light.

II.

Desire, carnal, tears away
from all that is sacred
and godly, flesh pinched
from divine marrow like
a hand seizing soft
parts in the ecstasy of
touch, of loving so much
a body you must believe
it has no end. What is holy
cannot be held in the ways
I might hold you
again. This is what I was told.

But, I don't believe it's true.
Has He not seen me grieve your body?
How I rescued your gym shirts
from the laundry basket
the day you died, to preserve the way
you were when warm, alive.

I've been on the tiles praying,
my hands feeling the cold, my cheek
pressed against the places you might be.
Surely He sees how much like Him
I become, trying to touch you
one more time.

Midpoint

The cow before the slaughter-
house chest-deep in mud
with shock, with legs
buckled hard in
not-prayer not-silence
between air and
buried

I remember being there
as much a nobody as
the cow

Tang of fear in my mouth
or something more certain

Bullet becoming
tongue

One touch, one drop
and there it is
the whole of you
draining away
white sheet fall ing
to the ground

When they came to tell me
you were dead
they didn't use those words

What do you think
they tell the cow
to get it to the shed?

All the way there
walking together
soft words

(come along,
that's it, good girl)

Warm hand at the edge

And there before the final door
the cow cannot walk,
cannot stand

Call me towards
the threshold

Whisper gentle
half-lies

(we don't know
where he is)

I, too, follow, don't know
where I am or who
is on ~~the floor~~
        the ground

One hand near my shoulder
less gentle
the steel in the cold
police fingertips
reaching through space-
time, squeezing
alarm
what do you mean
he wasn't feeling well

at what time did he
wake up did he
leave early did he say
where he was going

Ticking questions, casually
asking boxes

(what tattoos,
can I ask what
tattoos
did he have?)

The soil
the arms
marked with wings
his were
catching me
falling through

On a Cashmere and Lamb's Wool Mattress

I.

Of course everything is different now.
Do you think the King will greet him
at Horse Guards Parade, ask him to tea?
And he, who facilitated the bombing of
a maternity hospital, the razing of a city
right down to its last steelworks,
will smile politely as he says, Yes,
I take my tea with milk and sugar, thank you.
And later, he'll realise that nobody shook his hand,
and he'll think it was an archaic practice anyway,
and not think on it again, rolling over, deeper
into the folds of Irish linen, awash

in off-white.

II.

In my living room, god walks by—a small boy
freshly showered, his hair shining like a sleek cap
made just for him—and he asks, Mommy, what are they
saying on the news? It's nothing, I say.
It will all be back to normal soon.
And I change the channel to the cartoons.

When he sleeps, he takes up the whole bed,
and I watch his eyelids shielding me from something
very bright, rolling like the big bang
through his infinite mind. The idea,
just the idea of him: I can go on
without any answers, knowing nothing,

praying the whole time.

Leaving

the other
tasting, in fear, the
desolation of
survival
> Denise Levertov, *During a Son's Dangerous Illness*

He reaches up, hits his father's helmet
with balled up fists, a hundred times screaming
goodbye in a rage that is half-fight,
half-terrified, held within
his father's arms.
                              Rocking his son,
the soldier, removes a khaki glove to wipe away
tears and mucus with a bare hand,
leans to kiss the boy's reddened face, all
recorded for us in the West by a news reporter, who
zooms in on the father's head—the boy's flying
hands, and, terrible, godlike, narrates:
This boy seems to know what is to come
for his father, who must stay behind to defend
Mariupol against the Russians.

Any child knows, if you scream,
shout, hit, bite, scratch, tear, launch
yourself against the sky of
your father's arms
your mother's hair,
they will turn,
you will be seen,
and nobody will leave you
even if they're angry.

On the morning my husband
left for work and later

died, our toddler threw
himself into a wall,
banging his head,
a hundred times screaming *Daddy*
until I called down the long hallway
from our apartment   to the carpark, asking
my husband to return to us:
He's upset because you didn't say goodbye,
I said. And they hugged and.
Never. again.
Never.
Never touched again.

This is how a very young child
tries not to say goodbye
with the violent scratching at the sky
that sometimes adults too late
mimic   scratching at the soil
at their faces
at a body draped
in white cloth, at anything they can touch

saying with their fingers sharp
voice treble-hooked:
What has happened?
What is happening?

Carapace

The car accident happened at 20mph in a parking lot on campus.
The passenger side, where I sat, was struck, and I watched
the other driver through my window, her daydream cracking
like a cicada's exoskeleton as she realised what was happening,
the breeze coming in through the windshield all over her skin.
We could have made eye contact it was so close, so slow.
Shock can roll down the body like this: leisurely kiss along the shore,
and wondering where it might end—the gentle line of white-
wash they call *the break*.

You were driving me to a dance class before
the car accident, and I said: *It's ok, I can walk there. I still have time.*
You took me by my shoulders, and said close to my face: *Baby,*
you've been in an accident. You're not going to any dance class.
Everything seemed like A Big American Deal to me.
Eventually I agreed to stay, to provide a police report
on this very slow accident and let my idea of the future float away
for one evening. Later, we ate curry at a Thai restaurant
with a lopsided drive-through bay, faded image of a burrito
below the *Lotus Palace* sign. I stared at the sheen-black countertop
flecked with grains of rice, pale fingerprints, wondering:
Who really lost the plot?

The insurance company said our car—
with a single dented door—was a write-off. They paid
for us to see an osteopath, and when she asked how my neck pain
had started, I told her it was the car accident. She leaned
over her clipboard, ticked some boxes. Then her fingers
found the knots that were always there, always returned.
Not long after, you went away.
That last day, I was getting Raphael ready for the playground.
Holding him, trying to dress myself, strange fractals
of panic in my throat, and—a phone call that split

the seam of my life with its noise, white ringing in my ears.
For weeks I woke into the deserted bed,
two thoughts only in my head:
You had gone to work early in our new car.
I would meet you later on your lunchbreak.

Then your face a ghost up close to mine in the grey bedroom
the breeze dusting my shoulders from the open window
everything split wide—and something cold that was not
the air but my own skin, raw and not yet real—

But (*let me past you, I know where I'm going*)
if I can just lift Raphael over the crack,
we might reach the playground still,
find you waiting outside your office on campus at lunchtime.
It's ok, we can walk there. We still have time.

Remember falling in love

Remember falling in love. Remember
first breath held
for a whole lifetime

                                       it seemed
before that first kiss. Had I watched the ice cream drip—
ping down a cone and never tried to lean in
to it as a child on the scattered sand of the boardwalk
before this day? The kiss was there on my lips—
soft against soft, and love, falling through my skin, my eyelids,
into my lungs, so full now. I can breathe
again. The second breath. Why did you wait so long? Why
is everything grey
now that you are gone
and I must try to breathe

                                   like that

alone?

The calendar says, it is a new year.
The calendar says, it is a new year
twice. Some error. I inhale
slowly, cello bow rising up my skin,
key of C. I breathe still
like the ghost of you is
locked
somewhere in my lungs.
Back the bow comes down, hook
unclasped of sound, an exhalation—
what can you see, hear, feel, taste?
Another year I remember
standing alone, my head against a wall,
watching you walk across the black-and-white
of kitchen floor, some late party, some bare bulb

of light
and you before me leaning in—

Fireworks. Cockatoos light up the after-
midnight new day of the new year
with their brassy shock that this
(that this! that this!)
spectacle as bright as dawn is their waking gift.

Starlight as the synth, I breath
sharp
as some electric machine, some lonely song
at a rave for
the dead. Everyone has seen me naked
in my poems to you. Everyone
is asking how I feel. Jealousy
like the moment I thought you'd never reach me
across the kitchen,
you'd turn and take your perfect face far
away from me. All those years, you
breathing. And me, turning now,
finding my own face like a shock
of sound coming from a mirror.

Hello you,
you said.
Of course I couldn't move.

All the days.
All the days will pass
like this. Me breathing. You not

breathing.

On the other side of the moon, there is a kitchen.
There are white-and-black tiles. There is a bulb

bare as an eyeball, looking, looking—

Midnight and always
the wrong room again
the wrong room.

A SHARP PLACE

When I wake I find it is late autumn
     the hard rain has passed and the sunlight has not yet reached
the tips of the dark leaves that are their own shadows still
     and I am home it is coming back to me

       W.S. Merwin, *A Given Day*

All day I watch the sky changing from blue to blue.
For You are forever
and I am like a single day that passes.

     Mary Oliver, *More Beautiful than the Honey Locust Tree*
are the Words of the Lord

Fragments

I. Safe Place

In the night, I dream of people walking the streets
with flashlights. A group working together.
Daylight comes, and they are asleep where
nobody will find them.

II. Contingency

I say, *There is a security alarm.*
I say, *There is a child.*
I say, *There is a knife.*
But it's all out of order.
The first thing is the child.
The first thing is:
I know the limit is something I don't know.

III. School Drop-Off

Some days, I can't drive home
without him.

IV. Husband

I have a flashlight too, in this dream.
I'm alone. As long as I don't find him,
he's alive. As long as I sleep,
it's a dream.

V. Small

His bedroom is next to the front door.

These are the steps to take in an emergency,
or if he is coughing, fever-bright:
Lift him, move him to my bedroom.
Turn out the lights. Listen to him breathing,
and beyond? Maybe something, maybe nothing.
Animal-still. Cat. Fox.   Wolf—

VI. You

Would you say: *Leave,*
or would you say: *Please?*
In the dark, you don't know yourself.
There is a gap between the mirror and the bed
where you could hide your child.   You would whisper:
Do not make a sound,
your voice a line of fear cold as
the other side of the bed, the hall, the

front door.

VII. The Last Thing

He's the first thing. He's the first thing.

VIII. Bat

Daylight comes, and the nocturnal world folds
around its creatures. In the night,
I keep a flashlight near my hand because
I can't sleep because
I'm listening. In the day,
he finds the flashlight, flicks it—
off on off on maybe off—
who will know
until later? We rush along the road
to school, late again.

The dream is never long enough,
waking-falling onto the stage
through the velvet and the ropes
from the eaves into painful light.
The finite scapula, the crumpled silk of shock,
the stage lights now amber, now red, now—

IX. Meditation

Get up. There is nobody else.
Get up.

X. A Truth and Two Lies

There is a knife.
There is a security alarm.
I think I would say: *Please.*

XI. Please

Please at the corners of the mouth
like wings, triangles of black.
I know what the child would try to do
with the knife, near any man
who came near me.

XII. Cut

fruit for breakfast, cut bread
along the bias, cut the crusts, cut packets
so he can open them at school, cut the talking,
cut the driving-time by one minute, cut the corners
off the road with the wheels of the car, the tyres marked by isosceles-
indentations where someone lay soft in sleep against your
arm, the pressure of their collared pyjama-
shirt on the rubber of your skin.

XIII. Either/Or

Two things

The boy and his dead father.
The wolf and the knife.

that will not meet.

XIV. The Highest Shelf

To keep him safe.
Where I would never reach it in time.

XV. Dream

In the safe place, there is a flashlight
and a boy bright as a knife
hidden by my side.

The Helping Hand

My child, who is not from here, comes to talk
to me in my bedroom. My husband lies in
ashes on the bedside table and today is
his birthday, or it would be if I believed
in a heaven other than my son, might be
if I believed extra years of life were
somehow there accrued, in the cheerful way
of certain cheerful people who have wished
the eternal corridor of dead a *Happy Birthday
in Heaven.*

                    Not on my watch—
I mention his birthday to nobody, except
my child, who finds this idea a wonder,
miraculous even: a father who was once
alive and ate carrot cake.

                        My son
from far away, he comes to talk to me.
Some days I find him in my bedroom,
staring out at the pale sky, his head
tilted as if to ask a question of the blue
above: *But why?* they both say
to each other, endlessly agape,
the child, the sky, and me watching
from behind as if caught winded
in the middle.

                Today he holds, in one hand,
pages of a book he's written. In the other:
the stapler from my desk. I move away,
his daydreams too vivid to enter
with a basket of laundry at my hip.
When I pass by again,

he is in my bed
telling me the sheets are like the sky
outside and why don't I lie down too,
next to him and the trail of staples.
In fact, let the laundry unfold over us
as clouds.
                    It is good to undo chores,
to lie next to him in the fresh air
of his voice.
                    And how are you doing
in the sky, I ask my husband with
my eyes very far away, as my child
communes with God, in the way
he talks of things he cannot know.
Mommy,
                    this is my Helping Hand.
He raises his left hand. I turn now
back to him, my son inside the sky inside
my sheets. *Mommy,*
                    my Helping Hand
is a list of adults who could help me
in an emergency. You are number one
and number two. He closes two fingers.
If my daddy
                    were alive, he'd be on my list.
But if you fell on wet tiles, I couldn't
call him for help. So, I put our neighbour
John as number three. I could move
a chair next to the door to unlock it.
I could go to John's house and knock.
I know he's nice because he has a son
he drives everywhere. I hear them talking
when they park their car at night
near my window and you think
I'm asleep.

                                        My child,

he makes contingency plans. This
Helping Hand, this tell-tale
part where our life might come undone
across the floor. Everything is normal,
until it's not.

                                   This child,
this child right here, my only one:
he is definitely your son. Innocent and
pragmatic as any soldier sent to lift
the fallen.

                         When I shower as he sleeps,
or pretends to sleep, I step carefully.
Everything I do extends beyond me.
Steam rises through the window,
through the thick door of the night
to where you might be.

                              It is your birthday.
I am older than you. I would like to see
your face as it would be now. I would
like you not to see my face, but to lift
it and to kiss it, in the dark
as if I'm still the younger one.

In the bedroom, I watch your child
breathing deeply in sleep. I carry
socks to put away, teddy bears
picked up off the floor and—
other things, I forget
                    I forget all the things
I carry.
Look:

the sky
the sky is in the bedroom

in the bed. It has come in through
the window
as if it lives here all the time

a perfect blue unending
question—

to which there is no answer

only wonder, wide-
mouthed like waking

to a gift, to a birthday again
and again.

The Moon

I. Later

He thinks that I will die, and I wonder
what he knows. I study him one hundred
different ways when he's not looking at me.
I photograph him eating sliced oranges
because I like the way his eyelashes
are dark against his cheeks as
he looks down
and chooses the juiciest and the next
juiciest slice, all the way to the one he calls
the baby. My baby,

        he studies things too, little details.
        He is learning to swim. After
        his class, I take him into
        the deep pool. He holds
        onto the wall and peers down
        at me through the water.
        When I surface, he removes
        his goggles to talk: *Mommy,*
        in here you are small!
        When you swim, you look
        like a child moon-bouncing.
        Then he ripples away, not
        looking back, not yet able
        to swim alone. When he needs to
        breathe, I push him to the air, and
        I do this too often, just in case.
        His feet are shiny
        pearls trying to find the bottom,
        2.2m down. At night

he calls out to me
things a child should never say:
mommy be careful   mommy take care   mommy don't go outside at night
when I am asleep   mommy don't go into the garden in the dark   mommy stay safe
mommy check the door is locked mommy don't leave me mommy
where are you mommy can we be very old together—

and I never say:
gotosleep   doyouknowhowlateitis
whatisityouhaveseen(inme)inthedark—

His voice is so small

                                     so far away

with fear,
I can never reach him quickly
enough, and I know this is how
it will be when I die:
I will try to reach him and

forever

I will never get there.

II. Earlier

The carpark overlooks the swimming pool,
which overlooks the sea. We leave the car
in a hurry and descend the steps, tripping
three times. I hold his hand because
I know I make him walk too fast.
Somehow his class hasn't started
on time, and we appear to be early
at great cost. I wait with him until
he's in the water with his teacher.
I smile at her as if life is wonderful and,
Yes, we're early everywhere we go.

I tell him quietly, from the poolside:
I need to move the car. I will be back
in two minutes. But two minutes
is a very long time when you are five
in a swimming class, or when you are 34
and the carpark is full.

The pool is noisy with children
having fun, or perhaps in pain.
Beyond the pool, the waves break
across the shore, and the wind
whips the sand into a hard,
high sound that is ghostly.
Yet the day is sunny, and
this is a swimming pool
overlooking the beach.
Nobody here
thinks of ghosts. Above
the noise, I hear him. My skin
pricks before I identify the sound
with my ears. I press against the wall

high above the pool, and I look
down. He turns
in the water
and scans the audience of parents.
He doesn't see me
above him. His chest rises and
falls, a tide. His goggles float away

                                  electric blue

through the pool.

I'm here.
I'm right here.
I'm coming down—

I call again and

again
the waves break across the shore, and
the wind is a hard, high sound that
carries   my voice far

from his face, his lovely cheeks,
his eyelashes.

Daily Devotional

Did we start the day with hide-and-seek?
Did I tell him I love him by only letting
a count of ten pass
before I went searching for him?
Did I look for him in every shadowed corner
and not cease until I found him?
Did he laugh as if this was the greatest game,
to lie hidden, knowing he would be found
(as he was once within me and yet knew me)
by my voice?
Did I call out: 'Ready or not!' knowing
that he was ready, that the room stirred
not more than a whisper of hushed breathing?
Did he ever wait there and think I wouldn't
arrive?
Did we start the day with hide and seek?

Because I was worried that I would blink
and lose him,
I kept him in the bed next to me
against my own body
where once he grew.
In the night, he woke me:

Mommy, why are you crying?

His breath was as soft gauze
over my face, which was wet
from my eyes down past my cheeks.
I was in a cold sweat
drenched.

I was looking for daddy,
and I couldn't find him.

The same as hide-and-seek?

Yes, the same as hide-and-seek.
Only
when I saw you
could I stop looking.

Don't go back to sleep, Mommy.

I agreed it would be morning
then.
We rose and played
hide and seek
in the dark
again.
I laughed
like it was a game.

Circular Time

I can't say where the dagger falls
Precisely.

Sometimes it's always happening
                     Or it just happened
                            Or it was last week
                                  Two years ago.

It's like walking up steps
Carrying a child,
Little arms slung around your neck,
Remembering how you fell down the steps
In ice,
Clinging to the child to hold you up
With its preciousness
That you might never fall again.

Sometimes the child is older than me, more sensible,
Though he fits within my arms.
Or he's a toddler screaming: 'Mama! Love! Mama!'
When I cry for you, and I'm younger still, helpless on the floor.
Sometimes the child is grown up, and you and I are both gone,
And I have to walk into the cold chamber of that hypothetical
Because the child knows what Death is, and he doesn't know
How to hold a question back like you might half-cock a gun
And let the cartridge fall to the floor,
Safe from what the bullet wanted to say.
Sometimes the child is you.
And he lets me lay my head on his chest,
Which promises all the strength that you once had,
So that I might glance up
And think I've seen you,

Palimpsest of ghost on flesh,
If the angle of the light
And the slant of his cheekbones
Is just right.

The Wind

Imagine that I never spoke directly
to him,
that all I ever tried to touch was twigs
and leaves.
Imagine that, in passing, I brushed against him
every time,
preciousness I couldn't bear to grasp
or leave behind.

As the storm uncloaks itself out of
thin air,
I was so often on the cusp
of blowing up
with grief, so I kept myself away.

The wind can bring a sapling down
with force of fear,
with hands that crush by trying to hold
too much.
Some days, I couldn't look directly at him
for fear
my love would blow him
far
out of my reach.

I'd drive anywhere with you

We eat dinner in the car. I lock the doors
and then we're in the real world
of the two of us, inchoate in the half-dark
as surely it has always been somewhere
before here, and after, the accordion
of Time a trick, a thing you can compress
and stretch, and even sit inside.

I don't know how to say this any other way:
He's not from here. He's not like anyone
I've ever met.

He's so pleased I ordered him a double
cheeseburger tonight. *This is a once-a-month
treat. Fine dining*, I say. You should see his face.
He's six now, and he thinks this might go on
forever. This always growing up, these nights of
life contained and held. We read about Christopher Robin,
the real boy, while we eat. We discuss the shapes
that poems make, the little ones you can memorise
together in a moment in the car. Then I play for him
something new and also ancient: the sound from a black
hole. He says, *Oh*. And I say, *Yes, I know.*
I scroll the comments as the chasm speaks,
searching for the non-believer who will explain
away the chill running down my spine with
Simple Science. You can discount a lot of things
when you're not listening for a very particular
voice. I say, *Did you hear him?* And he says,
Yes.

Nothing needs to be explained between us.
Galaxies will collide one day,
Andromeda into the Milky Way.

We'll be long gone. The car, the drive-through,
the streetlights casting yellow orbs into the dark
like fishing nets. You don't know what's out there,
but you throw the line, and something moves—someone
echoes back, a Tuvan song, a life—a child asking me:
Will Heaven hit Andromeda too?
Like heaven might be somewhere here on earth,
like I might be the one who knows.

We'll be very far away by then, I say. *Picture*
a car with jet boosters. Picture a drive-through
in outer space. I'm in the front seat,
and you're in the back. What would you like to eat?

Through the black pool of night
we float, find all the world's asleep
except for us. There's a kind of magic on the edge
of normal family life: a singularity—
only we know what it's like.

At the traffic lights, I watch him in the rear-view mirror.
He's smiling. He's looking out at the sky, macadam
of gas and dust. *Can we do this again?* he asks.
I like our little chats in the car.

I nod. I watch the road. I watch the sky.
Nobody waits for us at home.
We could go anywhere.
We might go anywhere.

WATER SIGNS

Where the wind shreds prayers, on a dark
sea road, things loosen, lose

their form.
>   Felicity Plunkett, *Volta do Mar*

Swimming through dark, slow,
breaststroke—
>   not to startle
>   walls or chairs and
>   wake you—
>   Denise Levertov, *Love Poem*

Out of the Sea

I.

Because a child takes particular relish in revealing
a very good secret, he told me of the mermaid
in his dreams, but he called her The Woman in the Sea.
I wanted to stay with her beneath the waves,
he said, watching me carefully, as if unveiling
a pearl from beneath the layers of his
consciousness. My face was the axis on which
his faith spun, and when he saw my shock,
the gift receded quickly into folds of cloth—
Don't worry, Mum, she wasn't real.

II.

I too dreamed of the sea,
of walking out very far
into the waves.
I would be caught like an uncapped
bottle by the hands of the tide,
washed away, or washed up ashore—
it didn't matter which.
Already, I was drowning
daily, trying to keep going.

On the worst days, and especially during storms,
we went to the sea. The water moved as a scythe
back and forth, high and low, now blue, now black,
endlessly repeating—indifferently repeating
itself, itself across the shore.
There was a language which was neither grief
nor ignorance of grief. It was the sea.

III.

We walked in together. Always, it was this way:
the red bucket, the shovel shaped like a crab, and the boy
pulling me over the lonely sweep of bay into
the sea. A cup spilled across an infinite page, and the sky
shifted from blue to grey. The water carried away our warmth—
carried away our memory of warmth, lapping, leaning,
lifting our limbs, licking at our throats, whispering,
What more do you have? What else is there here?

We were near the Leeuwin Lighthouse, the rocky finger
of land reaching towards Antarctica. *You can touch
the bottom and not know there is another world
above*, he said, surfacing, clearing his goggles with
his thumbs, licking saltwater off his lips.

I lay in the waves watching shades of indigo
move across my eyelids,
deepest ocean from within.
He swam beside me and took my hand.
He said, *Mum, will you come under with me?*

At the red edge of the reef, he stopped, he pointed.
There was the creature—below us, penumbral as grief,
as the thing you fear rising from below. Half-scales, half-skin,
a shadow that became more real the harder he gripped my hand.

IV.

He gave me words with his eyes, so that I too watched—
or I was him, and turning, saw myself as he saw me:
the Woman in the Sea. *Yes, I saw her too,*
I said to him, when we were back on the sand,
breathing the hard, cold air into our lungs,
these things surely not made for us.

V.

If we dreamed, we dreamed together.
If we drowned, it would be me
dragging us both
down.

VI.

I don't know what to tell you.
I didn't write.
I didn't write for months.
The words were all inside me
and when I tried to talk
I cried,
as if water
might express
my longing to drown
better than words.

VII.

My child spoke that language too.
In the water, we talked.
The water was not only water.

We might go out there.
We might come back.
We might run up the dunes
breathing and breathing and learning
to breathe.

Koi

All the ocean in an eye
in water, a silvered flash,
its gaze a flat, pale disc,

a koi he coloured for me,
gold and sugared pink,

Frilled fin like lace fronds,
its eye a moon under moon

as fish on land. In my hand
a drawing, but in the eye
water, all the ocean.

a gift, to hold this fish,

this boy, this vast sliver
of me, carrying the sea.

an eye, blank and still

Buddhism for Mothers

Bees disturb the peace of pale sky
between pegged socks. The apiarist
I phone wants to know how many.
Far more are coming than going.
I wait for him. I focus on the wringing
of a sodden flannel, the scrubbing of oats
from a bowl I didn't soak—the meditation
left to me, too busy to *just breathe.*
But it is hard to meditate on chores
with the chant of bees around my head—
to fall into an eye-of the-swarm calm,
to measure a moving beast. I scrub
the bowl a little harder. Everything is tart,
the scent of lemons turned into dish soap.
Oh no! my son calls out. *Look at all
the bees in our garden, Mommy!*
Bees carrying nothing but themselves,
their loaded bodies, moving into a box
I couldn't store away. *Yes, I see them too,
darling. That box holds all your baby clothes.*
They rush in as if the box might soon reach
capacity, sharp in their striped suits,
their burglar's uniform dressed up.
One cloud, one swarm, one curtain billowing,
bound for the babysuits and lavender oil,
the bloom of so many sleepless nights.
There must be a message—biblical—
inside that box of baby scent and bees.
But I can't open it to find out. Now
they are chanting at the window,
and I am trying to work. Nothing
gets done but the little things,
and that's a day, day after day,
a cloud of them, a piece of the pale sky.

Only Parent, Only Child

Mommy, would you like to earn
marbles like I do, towards a reward?

Maybe it can be a family thing?
Being the only one who can

opt in, I agree—yes,
I will earn marbles too.

I make a Lego speedboat and
find I'm rich in glass marbles

with a citrus swirl like lemon
peel through the middle. Serving

vanilla custard for dessert
earns me another six: one prized

confection in beachball stripes,
three like dusky speckled eggs,

two dark as the space between
galaxies, orbed marvels of micro-

cosmos passed to me by small
hands, ever-expanding with love.

At bedtime, he escapes down
the hallway to sketch *just one more*

blue robot, five times over.
I find him in the half-light

drawing square heads and
rectangle bellies with urgency.

Exhaustion churns my words
into anger, clouded glass with

pinched strands of lime, and
shooters in devil's eye of carmine

or canary yellow, large enough
to knock aside smaller marbles.

After that outburst,
I lose all my marbles,

stripped of every single one,
which was the risk I took

because I am alive
and not everything I do is nice.

Don't worry, Mommy,
you can start again tomorrow.

Conversation

In the house we're going to build,
we'll have a pig—a pet— a little one.

*

I knew I wasn't going to school
because you were calm and smiling
at me from the sink.

*

No, we'll build a fence in the kitchen,
so he can't wander through the house
at night, and so he isn't cold in the garden.

*

I'm so glad to see you eating real food
with me.

*

I want a hammock in the garden and a tree house
with lava at the bottom. Like a moat.
Is lava real? How?

*

I thought of Wilbur. But also Ruby,
if it's a girl.

*

Both. How do you know?
Also, how is it made?

*

What size is a rat? How long is its tail?
And what shade exactly? Pink like
a fingernail, or pink like a rose?

*

Is a shadow the same as a silhouette?
Can a shadow come around a corner
first, before the thing—
the thing it is attached to?

*

He can eat with us in the kitchen.
If you only want to eat salad, it's ok.
We can give the scraps to Wilbur.

*

Some nights he might be lonely
in the dark after you go to bed,
after you've written your poems.

*

Is there a word for wanting tomorrow
to become yesterday?

*

Not moving forward.
I want to have today again.

Can it be Infinity?

I. Voyager 1

I didn't tell them when I fell,
he says. I can't find my tongue
to reply so I reach for his hand
and I steady him with my gaze

pressed tight. With my other
hand I wipe gently a full day
of sand from his knee once
bloodied but now—hours

after recess, lunch, Phys Ed—
no shade a knee should be.
Under the tap my voice
arrives a rush and maybe cold:

What are they teaching you
at school? And he says:
3D shapes, and he says:
Phonics, and he says:

How to watch the clock.
You mean how to tell the time?
Yes, he says, my mistake.
Pressed along the arc of

a paring knife, this is my curve
to learn: how to let him go,
how not to let him
break in doing so.

you would reach?
is the highest number
for your whole life, what
Mommy, if you kept counting

open as a window to the breeze:
against my cheek and I split
He is on his pillow whispering
lays me down flat to breathe.

the part that lifts me up,
backwards with its need. At last
the coming day pushing us
the clock. Late to bed again,

like I should learn to watch
I walk behind and watch him
galaxy, sideways and beautiful.
my son's paintings of the cartwheel

that it's a lot. We tour the class,
that two minutes has a cost,
greater than silence. We agree
phonics to convey an absence

these parts that don't add up, no
stop. There is no maths to explain
like my grief, a clock I couldn't
speak. I see her ticking over

II. Cut Knee

Parent-teacher night. We return
to school as if it is a game we like,
but always we are losing half-
lives, cusp of coping and cusp of

tripping up, the rush. On the drive
he draws Voyager 1 with eyes
and hands, a steering wheel.
See, Mommy, he can turn around

now. Vicious I become before
his teacher, a savage
uneducated in ways I couldn't
measure until tonight as she

asks me to set a timer for
my child when he is
eating, dressing, brushing
his baby-teeth. We run

late by maybe two to five
minutes on repeat. Alarmed
that we do not watch
the clock enough,

she plans a boot camp in
a language of egg timers.
My son orbits us, a
a second moon listening,

looping, moving into
shadow. His teacher says:
He daydreams, loses
focus, finishes last.

that makes it home. But I don't
alive, a dying spacecraft
my child won't have: a dad
over us. That's also a daydream

his life displaced like water
If I can't catch up, that's
of minutes two to five.
absence in tally marks

a father, I count out his
ision of a family without
the once. In the long div-
off only had to work

a rocket into space: take-
bravery of NASA shooting
made him keep trying,
the law of averages

less day. Something like
the span of a single end-
four different ways within
My husband tried to die

a drink, I want to say to her.
Sit down, pour yourself
becomes a dangerous thing.
every hot feeling now

of the sky of his mind,
anchored in the darkness
rising upwards to my child
Hydrogen encased in skin,

III. Hourglass, flipped over

Grey

.across the long grey-blue limpid line of
coast, smell of fire.

the mother reaching— —
and turning now
and still and whitely into light—

((and the child-
ren
now one voice calling
one

noise))

.at first lick all loveliness—gone.
.at.first.touch— —

—grey of Scotland, grey of dusk-gone-dark-
just, grey of heather shallow in the bay
and on the dunes, grey of lavender-ash where
blooms were sucked into the immortal
crime, grey of what was done and not done
enough, grey of babies' turning, turning to
their mother's black-grey eyes, grey of last look,
grey of grace of death of not-black not-white
not-living not-dead, last of all grey of dawn,
grey of the long and silent day when
they are not heard here
                              again
ever.

At evening and in the bay, the constant
grey that takes the vision, takes the breath
away
as if a ship in mist, as if a mother
turning—

voice tenderest tendril
last of all
last plume
the voice calling
still heard, still carried—

—as air inside the head, inside the ear,
for years, for all the years of anyone
who stood by watching the fire—
the day that lasted years—
and watched the turning and did not know
then
it doesn't end. Every mother turns, every mother
thinks—*Is that my child?*

HORIZON–MIRAGE

Your absence weighs more
than the stretch
          of your body
over mine

      Felicity Plunkett, *Interval*

everything is happening
at the wrong end of a very long tunnel.

      Richard Siken, *Straw House, Straw Dog*

Ruby-Throated

Leaning in, hummingbird over nectar,
Wings as heartbeats when you
So casually kissed me,
As if it was some
Everyday thing.

Hummingbird

I made you wings of paper
Shaped like aeroplanes,
Light as ashes.
I blew them up to you
Every time I blew a kiss.

With the wings I gave you
My grief moulded back
Into love, not heavy as sacred
Pillars of Herod's temple,
Destroyed where they stood.

They said I couldn't send
You love, that you weren't there
To receive it, so what I sent was still
Grief, a monolith like the Western
Stone of the Wailing Wall.

I said: Have you ever felt the breeze, diaphanous,
Dry your tears, as you gazed upon the sea?
Do you not think that is him kissing me
With his wings
In every beautiful thing I see?

first date

when I read
online
that you were
widowed
I knew you'd have
just
the right amount of
crazy
in you to let me do
whatever
I want, he said

and then The Crazy came out spilling across the table all over his black
    jeans where he had wiped
his hands as I walked to greet him
minutes earlier

At the Door

Down the legs dangle
and it moves just like a shadow
neither up nor down but steady
steady, smooth so that

if you saw it passing by
the window or your
shoulder you'd think it was
a watcher lurking

looking in at you
the way someone does
when they've imagined you
naked and now you are

in front of them
just some clothing in the way
then all that skin and
Oh, what do we have here—

The wasp moves on,
chandelier of sharp parts.
Of course a wasp doesn't hunt
like that. It's all chance

and opportunism.
But still.
Better to close the blinds.
Cover up the soft parts.

Second First Date

Carry me away from here
On your shoulders.
I think that if you looked back,
You would see that you forgot something.

He doesn't ask me about you,
He doesn't want to know that I write to you,
And I think there is something wrong with him.
I take a sip of water, my eyes slide to the roof
Of this cafe too small, too crowded
With waiters asking too often, too eagerly:
Is the food to your liking?
If I don't like the company,
Can I send it back?
I thought I asked for someone else.

I wipe my lips carefully with the napkin.
I have run out of words to drag
Like a smear of burgundy into the room.
I leave a smile sideways on my face
As if I might keel over unmoored, unbound,
Into my pappardelle if I weren't polite,
If I didn't complete a thing
That will never complete me.

Carry me away from here.
I want to bury my face in your shoulders
Like I used to when you slept
And you didn't know I needed you,
But you were there for me
Still.

Narcotic

If first I loved you, I go on now
giving the words of that language
to new men.
Between the speaker
and the listener, there is a gap
in meaning.
In that ravine, I take my refuge.
Nobody knows I'm down there,
still loving you, lying with
other men.

Here are the things I can give away:
clothes, unworn, in shades of oyster pink
like food that's on the cusp of spoilage;
spinning-top toys my son might have loved
had I not tidied them onto distant shelves;
books, never opened, on grief or trauma,
or some vicious combination of the two
('*Best Wishes,*' scrawled aslant, page ii).

At the back of the pantry, next to
vodka, cheap sauvignon from
the strata manager, and
stale chocolate elves,
are your tea bags, sealed
in a zip-lock bag.
Chamomile and valerian root.
Men come to visit me.
I like the sound the vodka makes
hitting the bottom of a crystal glass,
passing between our hands, glacial.
Your tea is hidden there,

would never be touched first
by them, who come here to see me,
touch me, as if we speak the same
first language.

I ask him if he wants tea after dinner,
like I always asked you, a mug
carried to you, the steam rising
in grassy tendrils to greet me
as I walked to you, to lie with you.
The scent now sealed away,
so I'm not taken by surprise.

I set his china cup in front of him,
keep your blue-brown pottery mug
pressed to my body, smile at him to say:
How nice you came to visit.

When I lay my head against his chest,
eyes towards the television,
it might even be you
I'm lying against, whispering to,
holding your mug,
drinking your tea, falling asleep,
your arms hoarding me.

Cut Glass

In a public space, with a child,
kindness and invasion merging
in one jaunty slash:
But how are you doing on your own/
are you managing alright alone?
These are questions that any
older woman in the milk aisle
or stranger at the playground
seems to consider
small talk.
Large enough to choke
on though. Maybe
the size of a marble: glass,
two fingers
                    down the throat
in width.

Sit down now. This part hurts,
always it is coming next,
like a punch after you've shaken
someone by their collar,
or imagined it and
let the fantasy show on your face
as a starting gun:
Have you met anyone else
yet?

How lightly they brush over
you, as if you might be
dust. I turn so they can see
my angles, acute
accents to catch the eye

sharply, my naked
mitre cut, split from its opposite.

Look, this part of me was ground
down like cliffs worn thin by sea.
I can't give it to another man.
He'll cut his hand, drop me.
I'll smash across the tiles.
It will look like I'm enjoying it
as he tries to walk away.

INTO HALF-LIGHT

It's not so terrible, she tells me,
not like you think: all darkness and silence.

> Dorianne Laux, *Death Comes to Me Again, a Girl*

Not the way long marriages are,
nothing happening again and again.
Not in the woods or in the fields.
Not in the cities. The painful love of being
permanently unhoused. Not color, but the stain.

> Jack Gilbert, *How to Love the Dead*

The Mirror

I.

When he comes for her, you know it will be you next.
He takes her hand lightly. He doesn't want to touch her,
but he's a doctor, and to some degree the bedside manner
makes the next part easier. She goes through heavy double
doors, which swing with their departure, leaving a small breeze
moving as a ripple across the lake of your heart.
Most doors in this place have small round windows—
portholes, to warn of someone approaching
from the other side. Oddly, the doors she passed through
have instead a mirror, but because you are seated,
and because your mind is on her—the way her lips
were white like glassine paper when she stood to leave,
polished with thirst, or fever —you don't notice
the absence of windows on this door. It is spring outside.
The perpetual winter of the hospital is the only god
you remember after one hour here. Two hours.
Three. Four. The doctor does not return for seven hours.
The length of a complex procedure. When he comes for you,
you are so tired from waiting—the thick plastic chairs,
the sterile air—you don't care where you're going. The white
space, the lacunae of the waiting room—it is in your lungs, your blood
cells. The doctor's starched coat matches the walls, so his arrival,
after all this time, takes you by surprise. In fact, you barely see him,
only make out his bared teeth, a smile. *Oh hello*, you say, rising, deferential.
He doesn't want to touch you, but—as with the woman—he must.
He leads you to the door by the edge of your fingers, grim and maybe
impatient. You are a man and haven't held hands with an adult male
since childhood. You think of your father, your brothers, your mother,
your son
who is now six, now alone with his own mother, your ex-wife,

who you remember in this moment as if you are still married.
Strange, strange shape of memory. Saying, *I will see you soon.*
And then you see your face in the mirror
as you cross the doorway, and the breeze moves across the lake
away from you, reaching to the other shore, the long arm of dusk—

II.

He stops drawing to watch his mother at the kitchen sink, her hands
hidden in the sheen of suds, her face towards the window, the fig tree
with its shrivelled fruit. Her left elbow makes the shape of an 'L,' her neck
is long, freckled on one side from driving, her hair falls in strands
from her ponytail. In a moment, she will turn her face from the window
to the boy. Her whole body will
follow, water will drip across the tiles from—

                                        The ripple
touches him first, carries him across the room shivering.
He almost slips, but she is picking him up and a sound
he has never heard before
arcs through her into him like broken glass.
Next she says, *Sorry. I'm so sorry. You gave me a shock.*
Something not possible
to speak
is pressed flat within the gap between their chests, tangible
as a piece of paper that will clearly state the facts.

III.

Kiss of two dark birds
at the edge of the lake. Evening,
pine trees cut from twilight as if by scissors, jagged
as a child's line of precision. Silhouette
of night closing like an absence around
the future.

IV.

The mother moves in front of the child,
the child moves in front of the mother.
The line of symmetry—of protection,
of warmth—can be in any direction.
This is how animals live.
This is how animals measure time:
What is here? What was here before?
At the axis there is need, which looks a lot
like love, which might be the same thing but

touch the glass, there's still a gap,
no way to send the paper back, to say year on year on
year: *I'm sorry, could you repeat that. I didn't hear you.*
Not a question. A statement of fact.

V.

Once you found a dead bird on the ground while walking
with your son. He was a toddler, small enough to inspect the bird
without kneeling. He tried to touch it, but you held his hand,
pulled him forward. You said: *The bird is sleeping.*

Bird is sleeping, he repeated the whole way back—
until every rock, every leaf, every brightly coloured
packet caught in the breeze had been told:
The bird is sleeping.

Wolfie

Then there is the reality
that I am not a robot,
and I go to my bed and I sleep
like my body is thirsty for the sheets.
Purple carpet, purple rain,
purple in my dreams again, and you
arriving to meet me right on time
like you never were in life.
A jacaranda bloom blows through the door
in front of you, and I pick it up,
feel purple flesh between thumb and forefinger.
The earlobe, the lip, the finger-tip.

Then there is the dog walking far
ahead of its owner in the steel-dark of the after-
dusk. The dog's head stills,
dips, sways—this way, that way—
slim dorsal fin invisible, and suddenly:
Oh there it is.
I see the thought swim through
the dog's mind—if I can call a vestibule
a room, for its body is already strung, already
reacting. In the air: the scent of people not there
anymore, but who had walked by
a minute or two earlier, carrying
food wrapped in folds of brown paper
to their door, to their house, to eat
without the dog, without the knowledge
of the dog
who is
now
waiting
on their doorstep,
salivating.

Then there is the poem in my head, the flesh
of the dream knocking at the vestibule
of my real life. The dog walks by and looks
at me, and tells me
with the low hum of his head to the ground
that he knows what I have dreamed,
that he knows
I am hungry too.

Then I am waiting
at the door with the dog. I go to bed a robot
metal-bent on some dream of finding hell,
of finding out what the humans mean
when they say, *I had the strangest dream.*
And at night you arrive
at last to take me on a date.
I say, *You've been gone a long time.*
And you say, *Where would you like to eat?*
Then we laugh and laugh because
we both know I'll go anywhere with you,
even into hell, Wolfie, even there,
my Love, if that's what you choose,
if that's what we call this dream when
soon I will have to

wake.

I say, *Come inside. It's five years
since you died. I think the burger place
round the corner might still be open
at this hour (by which I mean
these days—*

The door closes. The parentheses too.
The Dream is now
inside, looking at my phone,
checking reviews of old restaurants.

I lock the door. I say,
You're not going anywhere.
I show him my teeth.
I kiss him all over—softly, tenderly.
Earlobe, lip, finger-tip.
I am that sort of animal, and I want him to stay.
I say, *This is grief. I have lived as a robot*
for five years but
I'm coming back to life, if you will just
let me sleep.

Sea Glass

Once I called you crying from New Delhi Airport.
As soon as you answered, I knew it was a mistake.

Of course, everyone nearby could see what had happened:
I had been left behind. The WiFi dropped in and out,

taking your voice away at times, bringing it back
suddenly, as on a wave, on the shore of some blank coast.

Everything softens in time and space and—
I didn't know if you could hear me crying

each time the connection failed. When you answered,
your laughter, your wry smile came around the corner

of the world sharply. I had interrupted a conversation
with some funny person who was standing facing you

in the same room, listening quietly to me choking
every time you asked, *Hey baby, are you ok?*

So you were happy. Or distracted. And when I said,
I have to go, everyone in Duty Free is staring at me.

You said, *Who cares? You'll never see them again.*

Oculus

I.

They drive to the station together   for the last time
behind the broken glass of the windshield.
Everything is a risk until love ends. He says,
I have nothing left to lose, his voice rising tightly
to his throat like a fist   into the air
next to her face. But first. First there is despair,
salt of it sharp across her cheek.

Give the thing its name last of all. It might not end.
It might be a broken box, starlings leaving
formation like shards of window pulled free
of the frame, and the sky pouring in through the gap,
a terrible blue eye peering down
into a chasm. She stops the car. She kisses him.
She's says, *It's ok, I'll call you tomorrow.*

II.

The door closes and the car trembles and the glass
trembles, and she drives away with the wind
on her face. She's in a tunnel waiting for the train to pass.
Or she's a child, turning the handle of the car-window,
eyes closed to the dust rising off the freeway.
When she looks out again, she's home and
she can feel where his hand cupped her cheek.

Fugitive Pigment

Red tulips
living into their death
flushed with a wild blue
       Denise Levertov, *The Tulips*

I.

Through a doorway, there is a garden
with you at its edge. A row of cherry trees
lines the far wall. Your back is to me.
Raphael sits on your shoulders,
his arms raised to the low-slung fruit.

I am in the doorway, looking out.
Maybe this is the first still moment.

II.

You turn to me, rotating carefully,
sun dial carrying The Sun,
his lips stained bright, his red
fingers touching your temples,
the one dimple on your left cheek.
You reach to lift him
from your shoulders. A pause
where he's an extension
of you. Shadow-light,
the day coming always
undone, fading, failing,
hidden away.

III.

Behind you
the moon,
paper circle
made by a child,
not-quite-disc
of light.

This was where we lived.
Especially that garden,
especially in the evenings.
Albuquerque sky
every shade of pink
before it's blue.
Watermelon mountains
leaking pigment, flakes of
dusk blowing east.

IV.

And time
not really passing.
Just a trick
of light
that far from the tide.

V.

He clings to you, asks to be lifted
again. *Up,*
up, the only word he needs.
Meaning *love.*
Meaning *please.*

But I say it's getting dark.
The rest is gone,
is some other shade
I can't remember.

First and Third Stages of Grief

I have read it all searching for some
sign of you I will never find.
I even tried to write the words
myself, as if you might reply
in my own voice.

Here are the only words I want:
In the jungle, he was in time whole.

Give these to me and I'll set aside
my constant need to write. I will go
to the jungle, forsaking all others,
as I promised you once. But,
the words must appear only in this order:
He was in the jungle the whole time.

They will occur as a headline
in a newspaper article
I will never read
because I will by then
be on an aeroplane
from Western Australia

back to Peru
to find you still
alive—

and it is such a long,
long flight,
interminable as sky,
whole days gone in the middle
somewhere—

Lair

First the river like a gleaming snake. Later, the water in the air, the air heavy with moisture, so that you know the river is everywhere, moving in and all around like night coming down from the sky—smooth across your shoulders, your throat. But, first the river at a distance. Far below, umber of mud ensnaring its belly, vivid greens spilling across the land. Nothing is black or white, nothing is muted down there. High above it, you are suspended, watching every detail so intently it seems you're going nowhere, a mosquito over a coiled beast. Endless beating of the propellers, wings close behind, narrow span of fabric fastening your waist to the seat. And you know you have to descend from the sky towards the river. The only way back is down. Breathing slowly, quietly—a hunted creature acclimating to its fate. But your heart, it might have moved outside your body into the engine of this metal bird, as it considers where to settle.

On the ground, someone you don't know waits for you, smiling broadly at every foreigner, a placard waving like a flag. This is the edge of the Amazon, he says. He will drive you into the jungle, walk with you on the trail to the retreat. La selva, he enunciates, pointing beyond the town, a smile fraying across his face, some memory of a joke. People pass through this town on their way to other places. It is alive with movement—stray dogs brittle with suspicion and hunger, motorcycles carrying whole families, soccer balls taking flight beside traffic lights. Everything is pulled towards the green centre, the real centre, outside the town. Fruit trees line curbs that were never really there, dust and bricks giving way to life and more fissured life. Cacao farms and coffee plantations border the town, the traces of cultivation dispersing into vines and tendrils, serpentine green. Always, the jungle must be fought off. To live here at the edge is to mark time with the arc of the machete, the passing of years with the dance of green on green.

It is late when you pass the last expanse of cut grass that marks a soccer pitch, hemmed in by a few adobe homes. A white shape skims the horizon, launching out of the viscera of trees and leaves—perhaps a large bird, perhaps a small aircraft. Your guide drives you through the khaki-dark of the Amazon at dusk until there is no road, not even the gravel that becomes mud in the wet season. You exit the car towards something green and breathing, a wall of trees alive with eyes you sense but cannot see. The guide hands you a flashlight and moves into the darkness—velvet density of insects, white noise of the river hidden below. From time to time, scattered stars are visible above the halo of your flashlight. You remember watching the jungle from the aeroplane, the lustre of the canopy a scene from an oil painting, Rousseau's Dream stretching to the corners of the map. Now you are in it, sealed, sweating and heavy with the waxy air.

After an hour, maybe less, maybe more, you reach the hut. Not really a hut—a platform on stilts, built into the mud, thatched roof and wooden railing. Somebody will meet you after sunrise, your guide says. He passes a bottle of water to you, and nods goodbye, receding into formlessness. You unroll a mattress, lie down across the paths of ants, the unseen lives of creatures that don't sleep. Green bleeds into the dark all around, as if colour might be more than colour: autonomous, alive and looking back. Not a wall of night—a chasm, a mouth agape. The bottomless depth of the jungle without light. And you think, as if in prayer, *I can leave. I'm not from here. I can say I've changed my mind.* One flight, and the city sprawled to the limits of the sea wall. Low cloud and surfers flung across the long arm of the bay. Miraflores—mirage-city, dream-memory. This image lulls you to sleep that first night. You will ask, when you wake, to book a flight back to the coast. Nobody knows where you are, what you have left behind. And all the while it's already in you, in the air you breathe: the jungle holds close what it loves the most, feasting on decay.

In the morning, there is birdsong, and the chorus of the river over rocks and logs. Dawn light sifting through leaves. You walk downhill towards the river, hoping to find a path, a way to the other huts and other people. On the opposite bank, a spring of freshwater flows from a crevice in the rockface. Your feet slide through silt, ankle-deep, and you reach for vines to hold you up. You are laughing as you cross the river, fully clothed, as if it is a road on any normal morning. Maybe you will stay. Maybe you will eat the fruit and wait one more day. You breathe deeply, cup the water with your hands. It is cold, almost too sweet. And as you drink, the jungle uncoils inside you, has you dreaming you can leave, become somebody else, somewhere else, safe on the move. A hundred thousand lifetimes, a hundred thousand ways to seek the sky, a hundred thousand shades of green, and every shade decays. The river, always moving, always the same, ouroboros gliding towards its prey.

In Shadow

How many times to see
the moon rise
in a lifetime?
Not enough, whatever the number.
Out here, under the eye
of the moon, milk-bright,
I think of the darkness—
its other side
which still exists
though I can't see it.

In the dark
on the other side,
maybe it looks at you
just as I am looking
for you now—
turning
halfway
into the dark
to find the light.

After giving my deposition in your case

I felt very cold. I boiled water in the kettle
and poured it carefully down the neck of a hot water bottle.
I sat with the hot water bottle between my thighs.
I turned the heating up to 29 degrees Celsius,
and waited to be warm. After a while,
when I was still shivering, I made tea
with the leftover water in the kettle.
The house was quiet.
I could hear the leaves blowing across the pavement
in the courtyard beyond the window, and I wanted
to brush them up, but the cold outside was a wall—
my thought of the cold outside was a wall.
There was no way I could open the sliding door into
the space of reality—the world beyond the glass.

The cold inside took everything to carry,
and I knew it was you
not there
that I was feeling, as when somebody you love
very much
leaves the bed and there is a gap—

I talked about you as a dead person.
I trembled for hours.
What door had I opened inside myself
using those words, still thinking:
He might return. Do I tell the lawyer—
he might return?

Leave me to my dreams.
Or come back and
close the door behind you.
I'll wake up. I'll know it's you.

The Lamb

I.

My first boyfriend messaged me
asking if I'd like to meet
for coffee. We've been messaging
for months, and today
it is six years since
your last day of life.

There is an animal in our house now
that finds me when I'm happy
and asks me to carry it everywhere,
softly bleating if I bend
to set it down.

Even holding the lamb carefully
against my chest,
I said yes. It could see me typing,
and looked up at me, as if knowing
from my face, my eyes, my hands
what sort of person I am, who carries it,
who lies next to it in the dark
when it is dreaming and most vulnerable
night after night.

Yes, I replied at 2am,
watching the lamb watching me
with its huge eyes dark in the bedroom.
Yes, I'd like to meet you.

II.

The lamb is on my lap as I sit
in the passenger seat.
I held it as I dressed to meet this man
who came before you, who knew me once
when I was reliable, when I didn't have
this problem
indivisible and heavy
in my hands everywhere I go.

Safety blows in through the open window
of the car and makes me shiver.
How long since I have been a passenger
in somebody else's car?
How awful to sit here calmly,
to let him think I'm happy to see him.

Once he, too, had left forever, it seemed,
and, out of the blue, he returned.

III.

The lamb needs me,
and I cannot set it down.
I held it against my hip
as I put on eyeliner, mascara, concealer,
as I pulled my hair up off my neck,
took the green dress from the wardrobe.
Not the one you loved, but similar.

Things like this happen.
People come back from almost-death
and send messages and ask to meet,
knocking at the door after years
and hours apart.

IV.

If I tell him not to come again, he'll ask,
What's wrong? If I message him to explain,
he will reply. He might take some time,
but he will reply.

V.

I want you to know I will take care of the lamb.
I don't mind it being here, most of the time,
and I know you would come to take it away
if you could.

Afterword

You're My Best Friend

I turn on *You're My Best Friend* by Queen as I eat dinner, and he sits beside me on the floor constructing a wonderland for miniature cars, each with their own distinct character, which he voices in low tones. I say to him, 'This is for you.'

Do you sit beside him on the floor as he waits for me? All the hours he would be left waiting, alone, but for his spectacular imagination, did anybody think to tally those up before they pulled your card? There must be enough of those hours now to get him free entry into Heaven (whatever shape that takes). A sort of grace for all the fatherless children, a back-handed clemency.

Once he said to me, 'I don't have a dad.' It was a child's statement of fact as observed, not intended to bring me to my knees. Kids in his preschool class were making Father's Day cards to present to their fathers who would stand in the classroom at morning tea. What he meant with those words was: 'I don't have a dad to stand in the classroom and share morning tea with me.'

Now I tell him all the time, as one might recite a prayer, 'You have a father, he's just not here in his body.' It sounds like you've been injured and must be kept at a distance to coalesce. He teasingly calls me *Mommy-Daddy*, and we pretend I have a split personality, veering from the booming tones of a father to the soothing tones of a mother. Except that's not make-believe. I must be both. I can't be both. I am both.

I want him to know you loved him, you wanted him. This distinction must be knit within his soul so deeply he can't doubt the worth of his own being, the heavy weight of fabric without price. There are worse things that haunt those with absent fathers than waiting on a mother doing everything at once all the time every day ever on including voicing characters for miniature cars while making school lunches in between cooking pasta pushed aside to fold laundry on the countertop and heaven forbid she should stop to eat her own food or even for a second   breathe.

I turn on *You're My Best Friend* by Queen as I eat dinner, and he sits beside me on the floor constructing a wonderland for miniature cars, each with their own distinct character, which he voices in low tones. I say to him, 'This is for you.' He is quiet, briefly.

Did you know you were my best friend too? Some nights (all the nights, always) I'd really like to talk to you. We used to tell each other everything. Except for that one last thing you (haphazardly) planned to do. You never mentioned that.

When he's peaceful, in some place of childlike wonder that is at once miraculous and fundamentally quotidian (like right now), I can see you sitting next to him on the floor. I don't think he knows you're there, but you are both my best friends. You would have been best friends, you and him, if you'd had a few extra years.

I turn on *You're My Best Friend* by Queen as I eat dinner, and he sits beside me on the floor constructing a wonderland for miniature cars, each with their own distinct character, which he voices in low tones. I say to him, 'This is for you.' He is quiet, briefly, looking away. He doesn't see that I cry for my other best friend. You're with him there, in his imagination, in all the miraculous things he does as if they're commonplace, natural, just the way he was made, the best parts of you, of me, of words we never got to speak into being.

In the beginning, was the Word, and the Word was with God, and the Word was God. I think of that line a lot in relation to him. Through him, we're both redeemed, and yes he's holy to me, and he's also a normal kid who can push every short-fused button tucked away inside my wiring. And I wanted to be full of grace, to be calm under pressure like wax refusing to melt before a flame. But he taught me grace has nothing to do with how you move, with how you look as you come undone. He can be words that bring life like light into sunless spaces. He can be the last candle in a world of dark, after I said the light—the happy parts—hurt my eyes and must be blacked out. He can cause me to crumble, bring me to my knees, and he is the only one who can pull me up, though he is smaller than me, for now. *I know I'll never be lonely, he's my only one.* Just like you were.

In the end too, the Word is there, both with god and the embodiment of god. He can be a man, a small boy, a best friend, because all he is—and he is all to me—is love. The sun and the wax. The heat and the melting. The feathers aflame with light, and most of all the flight: the prayer sent through smoke and ash, soaring into the dark—vast tendril, infinite thread.

Notes

On a Cashmere and Lamb's Wool Mattress

1. This poem refers to the siege of Mariupol, which occurred between February 24 and May 20, 2022, and which formed a major component of Russia's initial offensive in the Ukraine.

2. Furnishings described in the poem feature in the household of the English royal family.

Leaving

1. This poem also makes references to events from Russia's attack on the Ukraine in May 2022.

I'd drive anywhere with you

1. This poem makes reference to 'Now We Are Six,' by A.A. Milne.

2. On singularities in the context of astronomy: 'Singularities are regions of space where the density of matter, or the curvature of spacetime, becomes infinite. In such locales, the standard concepts of space and time cease to have any meaning' (astronomy.swin.edu.au).

Grey

1. This poem makes reference to the murder of Macduff's family portrayed in Shakespeare's *Macbeth*. In particular, this poem addresses a scene from the 2015 film adaptation of the play, directed by Justin Kurzel. It is a scene that I found immensely difficult to watch, due to the nature of my husband's death. The poem arose in my mind as a complete sequence while I was turned away from the screen.

Acknowledgements

The writing of this collection wouldn't have been possible without support from my family, my friends, and the writing community. In particular, thank you to my mother, Marie, and my parents-in-law, Irene and Sigi, who gave me time and space to write by caring for Raphael. Thank you to my father and brothers for indulging my love of words and stories, going way back. Immense gratitude to my mentors—Gwyneth Lewis, Diana Spechler, Peter Streckfus, and especially Felicity Plunkett, who knows so well the life I live, writing in the pockets between caregiving. Your encouragement and artistic kinship are precious to me beyond measure, Felicity. Thank you also to my editor, Penelope Layland, for your belief in this manuscript, and for your compassionate editorial guidance. And to my publisher Shane Strange: thank you for giving me this opportunity, and for your artistic vision—you've transformed my belief in what is possible, ever after.

Finally, thank you to Raphael—I couldn't do any of this without you, my angel. You're the one who is always there, late at night, early in the morning, when I feel heavy with grief or despair: you are by my side. When I see your face, I remember how lucky I am—to live every day with you—and I can keep going. I hope one day, when you are much older, you read these poems and know how loved you are, how loved you always were, by me and your father. He exists still in this world, in all the lovely, funny, daring parts of you.

Questions was published in *Cordite Poetry Review* (Issue 103: Amble).

Rain Lilies was shortlisted for the Newcastle Poetry Prize 2022 and published in the prize anthology.

Hunter Green was Highly Commended in the Calanthe Press Poetry Prize and published on their website.

Lake was published in *Cordite Poetry Review* (Issue 106: Open).

The See-Through Friend was published in *The Suburban Review* (Issue 26: Revel).

On a Cashmere and Lamb's Wool Mattress was shortlisted for the ACU Poetry Prize 2022 and published in the prize anthology.

Carapace was Commended in the W.B. Yeats Poetry Prize 2022, and later published in the *Grieve 2022* Anthology.

Fragments was shortlisted for the Newcastle Poetry Prize 2023 (final decision to be announced).

Circular Time was published in *Westerly* 65.2 (November 2020).

Daily Devotional was published in *Australian Poetry Anthology* Vol. 9, 2021.

Buddhism for Mothers was published in *The Weekend Australian* of October 30, 2021 (featured in the Books section of the Review).

I'd drive anywhere with you was published in Rattle Magazine's *Tribute to Irish Poets* (March 2023).

Second First Date and *Narcotic* were published (under different titles) in the *Poetry D'Amour 2021* Anthology.

You're My Best Friend and *Koi* were published in *Limina Journal* (Issue 27.1).

Ruby-Throated Hummingbird was published in the *Grieve 2021* Anthology.

About the Author

Kerry Greer is an award-winning poet and writer based in Western Australia. She received the Venie Holmgren Prize for Environmental Poetry in 2021. Kerry has been shortlisted for the ABR Calibre Essay Prize, the Stuart Hadow Short Story Prize, the Woollahra Digital Literary Award, the Newcastle Poetry Prize, the ACU Poetry Prize, the W.B. Yeats Poetry Prize, the Bruce Dawe Poetry Prize, and more. In 2022, she was one of ten writers selected for the Publishable program, run by Queensland Writers Centre. She was longlisted for the Publishable program for a separate manuscript in 2023. As a widow and solo parent, Kerry has a particular interest in writing about grief and what comes after loss.

Kerry was born in Northern Ireland, and moved to Western Australia as a child. She has also lived at length in New Mexico. She completed a B.A. in English Literature and French at the University of Western Australia in 2008. She is an MFA candidate in the low-residency program at Cedar Crest College. Kerry has received mentorship from Welsh poet laureate Gwyneth Lewis, Australian poet and academic Felicity Plunkett, and U.S. poet Peter Streckfus. She participated in a writing residency in Barcelona during July 2022, and in Vienna during July 2023.

Kerry's work been widely published in literary journals and anthologies, including *Meanjin, Westerly, Cordite Poetry Review, Australian Poetry Journal, The Weekend Australian Review, Plumwood Mountain Journal, Rabbit, Grieve Anthology,* and more. Her fiction was published in *ACE III: Arresting Contemporary Stories by Emerging Writers* (Recent Work Press). Her poetry features in a tribute to Irish writers published by *Rattle Magazine* in March 2023.

Kerry was awarded a micro-residency to work on new material during the 2023 Perth Poetry Festival. She performed material from her residency at the Festival Finale. She has also performed her poetry at events online and in Australia.

www.ingramcontent.com/pod-product-compliance
Ingram Content Group Australia Pty Ltd
76 Discovery Rd, Dandenong South VIC 3175, AU
AUHW020721050325
407891AU00005B/38